Table Of Contents

From Start-Up to Speed: A Step-by-Step Guide to Launching Your Turo Car Rental Business

Chapter 1: Understanding the Turo Car Rental Business

What is Turo?

Turo is a peer-to-peer car rental platform that allows individuals to rent out their personal vehicles to others. It offers a unique and innovative way for people to make money by sharing their cars with those in need of transportation. Turo has gained popularity in recent years as an alternative to traditional car rental services, providing customers with a wider range of options and flexibility.

For entrepreneurs looking to start a Turo car rental business, understanding the platform is crucial. Turo allows owners to list their vehicles on the platform, set their own prices, and manage bookings through the app or website. It provides a convenient way for owners to monetize their cars when they are not in use, making it a lucrative opportunity for those with idle vehicles.

One of the key benefits of Turo is its flexibility for both owners and renters. Owners can choose when and where to rent out their cars, while renters have access to a wide range of vehicles at competitive prices. This flexibility has made Turo a popular choice for both business and leisure travelers looking for affordable and convenient transportation options.

By understanding what Turo is and how it works, entrepreneurs can capitalize on this growing trend and launch a successful car rental business. With the right strategies and marketing techniques, entrepreneurs can attract customers and grow their Turo business into a profitable venture. In the following chapters, we will explore the steps to launching and growing a Turo car rental business, providing valuable insights and tips for success in this industry.

The Benefits of Starting a Turo Car Rental Business

As an entrepreneur looking to break into the lucrative world of car rentals, starting a Turo car rental business offers a unique set of benefits that can help you quickly establish yourself in the market. Turo, often referred to as the "Airbnb for cars," allows individuals to rent out their personal vehicles to others, providing a flexible and cost-effective alternative to traditional car rental companies.

One of the key benefits of starting a Turo car rental business is the low barrier to entry. Unlike traditional car rental companies that require significant capital investment in purchasing and maintaining a fleet of vehicles, Turo allows you to start your business with just one or two cars. This makes it an ideal option for entrepreneurs looking to dip their toes into the car rental industry without committing to a large financial outlay.

Additionally, Turo offers a unique opportunity for entrepreneurs to tap into a growing market of consumers looking for affordable and convenient transportation options. With Turo, you can cater to a diverse range of customers, from budget-conscious travelers to luxury car enthusiasts, allowing you to tailor your offerings to meet the needs of different segments of the market.

Furthermore, starting a Turo car rental business allows you to take advantage of the sharing economy trend, which is increasingly popular among consumers seeking more sustainable and community-driven alternatives to traditional ownership models. By participating in the sharing economy through Turo, you can not only generate additional income by renting out your own vehicles but also contribute to a more sustainable and environmentally friendly mode of transportation.

In conclusion, the benefits of starting a Turo car rental business are numerous, from the low barrier to entry and the flexibility to cater to different market segments to the opportunity to participate in the sharing economy. If you're an entrepreneur looking to launch a successful car rental business, Turo offers a promising platform to help you achieve your goals.

Market Analysis: Is There a Demand for Turo in Your Area?

Before diving headfirst into launching your Turo car rental business, it's essential to assess the demand for such a service in your area. Conducting a thorough market analysis will help you determine if there is a viable market for Turo rentals and if your business is likely to succeed in your chosen location.

Start by researching the demographics of your area. Is there a significant population of tech-savvy individuals who are likely to embrace the concept of peer-to-peer car rentals? Are there frequent travelers or tourists who may be interested in renting a car through Turo instead of traditional rental agencies? Understanding the characteristics of your target market will help you tailor your marketing strategies to attract potential customers.

My Turo is located near New Orleans, Louisiana. According to data from NewOrleansCityBusiness.com, the Louis Armstrong New Orleans International Airport recorded a significant increase in total enplaned passengers, with numbers updated through Sept. 30, 2023. In 2023, the total enplaned passengers year-to-date reached 4.6 million, marking an 8.5% rise from the 4.3 million passengers in 2022. This upward trend suggests a robust market potential for Turo hosts in New Orleans.

Next, look into the competition in your area. Are there already established Turo hosts offering a similar service? If so, what sets your business apart from the competition?

You can easily look into competition in your local area by going to Turo.com or the Turo app and doing a quick search in your local area.

Consider conducting a SWOT analysis to identify your strengths, weaknesses, opportunities, and threats in the market. This will help you develop a unique selling proposition that differentiates your business and attracts customers.

Additionally, consider the regulatory environment in your area. Are there any specific regulations or licensing requirements for operating a Turo car rental business? Make sure you are in compliance with all legal requirements to avoid any potential obstacles down the road. Most states have a motor vehicle commission that regulates licensing requirements in their state. Please be sure to contact your local motor vehicle commission for specific regulations or licensing requirements in your state.

By thoroughly analyzing the market demand for Turo in your area, you can make an informed decision about whether to proceed with launching your business. Remember, success in the Turo car rental industry relies on understanding your market and meeting the needs of your customers.

Chapter 2: Getting Started with Your Turo Car Rental Business

Setting Up Your Turo Account

As an entrepreneur looking to launch your Turo car rental business, setting up your Turo account is a crucial first step. Turo is a popular peer-to-peer car sharing platform that allows individuals to rent out their vehicles to others, making it a great opportunity for those looking to start a car rental business without the high costs associated with traditional rental companies.

To set up your Turo account, you will need to go to the Turo website or download the Turo app on your smartphone. From there, you will be prompted to create an account by providing some basic information such as your name, email address, and password.

Be sure to confirm you meet the age requirements to list your vehicle with Turo. US, Australia and Canada hosts must be at least 21 years old. UK hosts must be at least 18 years old to list in ABI 1-50. Hosts in all countries must also meet the following requirements:

- Have valid car insurance
- Meet legal and insurance standards and requirements for your region
- Follow our Turo's Exclusivity policy (US and Australia hosts only)
- Check vehicle eligibility requirements

If your vehicle is financed by a bank or other financing institution, be sure to review the language of your lease or financing documents to confirm permission to list your vehicle on a car sharing platform. Hosts in UK and Australia must obtain additional permissions if their vehicles are financed.

Once your account is created, you can start listing your vehicles for trips.

When setting up your Turo account, it is important to carefully fill out all the necessary information about your vehicles, including photos, descriptions, and availability. This will help potential renters get a clear idea of what you have to offer and increase your chances of getting bookings.

Additionally, be sure to set competitive prices for your rentals based on factors such as the make and model of your vehicles, their condition, and the market demand in your area. Be sure to check Turo.com or the Turo app for current going rates in your area. Offering discounts, promotions, or special deals can also help attract more renters and build your reputation on the platform.

By setting up your Turo account properly and effectively managing your listings, you can maximize your earning potential and establish a successful car rental business on Turo. Stay tuned for the next chapter on how to promote your listings and attract more customers to your Turo business.

Creating an Attractive Listing

Creating an attractive listing is essential when it comes to running a successful Turo car rental business. Your listing is the first thing potential customers will see, so it's important to make a good impression. Here are some tips to help you create a listing that will attract customers and set you apart from the competition.

First and foremost, be sure to include high-quality photos of your car. Customers want to see what they are getting before they book, so make sure your photos are clear, well-lit, and show off the best features of your car.

Please note that Turo automatically crops your images by about 20% when you upload to your listing. It is recommended that you take 5 to 7 steps back to shoot an image each time. This will ensure there is enough extra space around the area you are capturing in the photo so that it is fully visible in your listing.

Take at least 10 photos from various angles capturing both the interior and exterior. Be sure to take photos of any extras you offer in your listing such as coolers, child safety seats, tents, or other gear items. No stock photos are allowed on the Turo platform. Consider hiring a professional photographer to take photos if necessary.

Turo may restrict your vehicle listing if you include any of the following in your photos:

- Text overlay or censorship/black bars
- Stock images
- Lewd or indecent content
- Markings and advertisements, including advertisements from other car-sharing sites
- Photos that feature towing
- Inappropriate, hateful, or discriminatory symbolism

Next, make sure your listing is detailed and informative. Be sure to have handy all the relevant information about your vehicle, including:

- License plate number
- Vehicle make, model, and year
- Vehicle Identification Number (VIN)
- Detailed vehicle description of your car, including what's great about it and why guests would love traveling in it

Be sure to also include information about your pricing, availability, and any rules or restrictions you may have for renters. Do not share personal information like phone number, address, or social media in your listing.

In addition to providing detailed information, be sure to highlight what makes your car unique. Do you offer free delivery? Do you provide a car wash before each rental? Make sure to mention these perks in your listing to attract customers.

Finally, be sure to keep your listing up to date. Update your photos, pricing, and availability regularly to ensure that your listing is always current and accurate.

By following these tips, you can create an attractive listing that will help you stand out in the competitive Turo car rental business. Remember, first impressions are key, so make sure your listing is the best it can be to attract customers and grow your business.

Pricing Your Rentals Competitively

When it comes to running a successful Turo car rental business, pricing your rentals competitively is essential. Setting the right prices can attract more customers, increase your bookings, and ultimately boost your profits. Here are some tips to help you price your rentals effectively:

1. Research the Market: Before setting your prices, it's crucial to research the market and see what your competitors are charging for similar vehicles. Take into account factors such as location, car model, and amenities to determine a competitive price range for your rentals.

2. Consider Your Costs: Calculate all your expenses, including the cost of purchasing or leasing the vehicle, insurance, maintenance, cleaning, and other overhead costs. Make sure to factor in a reasonable profit margin when setting your prices.

3. Offer Competitive Rates: To attract more customers, consider offering competitive rates compared to traditional car rental companies. You can also offer discounts for longer rental periods or special promotions to entice new customers.

4. Monitor Demand: Keep track of your booking rates and adjust your prices accordingly based on demand. During peak seasons or holidays, you can increase your prices to maximize profits, while offering discounts during slow periods to attract more customers.

5. Provide Value: To justify your prices, make sure to provide value-added services such as complimentary insurance, roadside assistance, and flexible pick-up and drop-off options. This will help differentiate your rentals from the competition and justify your pricing strategy.

Turo gives you options for setting your vehicle price and lets you modify prices for a single vehicle or an entire fleet. The pricing options include **Automatic Pricing**, **Pricing Insights**, **Custom Pricing** , **Last-Minute Boost Pricing** and **Discounts**.

Turo opts all new vehicle listings in the US, Canada, and the UK into **Automatic Pricing** when available. Automatic Pricing adjusts the vehicle's price based on vehicle type, location, trip history, and changes in supply and demand. Automatic Pricing adjusts within the minimum and maximum price range Turo has set for your vehicle, based on its value.

In a vehicle's listing hosts can go to the Pricing and discounts page to turn Automatic Pricing off or on by using the toggle switch. When turning off Automatic Pricing you must manually set your own Daily price. When turning on Automatic Pricing you must manually set your own Price range, and your minimum and maximum price must fall within the pricing limits Turo established for your vehicle.

Limits are based on the vehicle's value and can not be changed. The changes will be applied to all new requests. Prices will remain the same for any previously booked trips and existing requests.

Hosts who want to manually set their vehicle price can utilize Turo's **Pricing Insights**. When you open a vehicle's calendar in the Turo app, you will be prompted to "Swipe up for more insights" to see pricing trends for vehicles that match or are similar to yours. The app will show the median weekday and weekend booked price trends.

You can check these trends to see how your vehicle's price compares to other vehicles offered by Turo hosts in your area and use them to guide your pricing decisions. Turo updates trend data at the start of every month.

Custom Pricing may be used as desired. Turo hosts can set different prices for different days of the week in a vehicle's "Pricing and discounts" section or for multiple vehicles and/or date using the calendar under the Trips tab. Custom Pricing overrides Automatic Pricing.

Turo opts all new listings into 5% last-minute **Boost Pricing**. This feature automatically boosts vehicle prices for same-day bookings if hosts have set their Advance notice to less than 24 hours. You can increase, add, or remove last-minute boost pricing at any time.

Turo hosts can also offer guests **Discounts** to entice guests to book their vehicles. You can offer early bird and trip duration discounts. You can also send post-trip discount codes to encourage repeat bookings.

Turo opts all vehicle listings into offering a 5% early bird discount for trips booked one week or more in advance. Hosts can increase the discount to 10% or remove it at any time.

Turo opts all new vehicle listings into all trip duration discounts (three days, one week, two weeks, one month, and two months). To set, change, or remove a discount, hosts can navigate to the "Pricing & discounts" tab in the vehicle's listing. A three-day discount must be lower than a one-week discount, a one-week discount must be lower than a one-month discount, and so on.

Hosts can encourage guests to rebook with them by sending them a 5%, 10%, or 15% discount code after they complete a trip in one of their vehicles. Discount codes are one-time use only, non-transferable, and valid for a trip in any of your listed vehicles up to 90 days after the guest receives it. The discount percentage is applied to the next booked trip's price, up to a maximum of $100 off.

An individual discount code can be combined with early bird and trip duration discounts. Turo gives hosts the option to send a discount code when Turo prompts hosts to rate their guest's trip.

By pricing your rentals competitively, you can attract more customers, increase your bookings, and build a successful Turo car rental business.

Stay updated on market trends, monitor your competition, and provide exceptional value to ensure that your pricing strategy is effective and profitable.

Chapter 3: Building Your Fleet

Sourcing Vehicles for Your Turo Fleet

As an entrepreneur looking to launch your Turo car rental business, one of the most important steps is sourcing vehicles for your fleet. The vehicles you choose will ultimately determine the success of your business, so it's crucial to make informed decisions when selecting cars to offer to your customers.

When sourcing vehicles for your fleet, there are a few key factors to consider. First and foremost, you'll want to choose cars that are in high demand and popular among Turo users. Conduct market research to understand what types of vehicles are most commonly rented out on the platform and tailor your fleet to meet those preferences.

Additionally, consider the age and condition of the vehicles you're considering adding to your fleet. While it may be tempting to purchase older, cheaper cars to save money upfront, keep in mind that these vehicles may require more maintenance and repairs in the long run. Opt for newer, well-maintained cars that are less likely to break down and cause disruptions in your rental business.

When sourcing vehicles, also consider the insurance costs associated with each car. Insurance is a significant expense for Turo hosts, so be sure to factor these costs into your budget when deciding which vehicles to add to your fleet. Look for cars with lower insurance premiums to help maximize your profitability.

A potential excellent source of vehicles is dealer auctions. However, you must become a licensed vehicle dealer in your state to have access to dealer auctions. Please be sure to contact your local motor vehicle commission for the specific vehicle dealer licensing requirements in your state. Most states have minimum requirements including:

- Completing an application
- Completing a training course
- Obtaining a surety bond
- Obtaining garage liability insurance
- Obtaining daily rental insurance
- Zoning verification for your location
- A business sign for your location
- A business sign for your location

Dealer auctions with a national presence include Manheim (www.Manheim.com), ACV Auctions (www.acvauctions.com), and ADESA (www.adesa.com).

Turo partnered with dealerships, car retailers, and car manufacturers with financing offers for Turo hosts to help you buy additional new or used vehicles to add to their inventory.

Turo's vehicle sourcing partners include:

- **Davis Smith Motors**(https://www.davesmith.com/turo.htm)

- **Auto Nation**(www.autonation.com/special-autonation-offer-turo-hosts)

- **Nissan** (www.nissanusa.com/dealer-locator.html)

Lastly, don't forget to consider the logistics of managing a diverse fleet of vehicles. Think about how you'll store, maintain, and clean each car in your fleet to ensure they're always in top condition for your customers.

By carefully sourcing vehicles for your Turo fleet, you'll be setting yourself up for success in the competitive world of car rental entrepreneurship. Make informed decisions, consider the preferences of Turo users, and prioritize quality and reliability when selecting cars for your fleet.

Financing Your Vehicles

As you grow your Turo car rental business, you will likely require access to funding to acquire more inventory. Turo has partnered with several auto lenders offering vehicle financing for Turo hosts to help them grow their business.

- **Automotive Finance Corporation** (www.autofinance.com/mobility) is offering lines of credit starting at $50,000 to qualifying Turo hosts with a registered Business (LLC, C-Corp, S-Corp or Partnership). The credit lines allow hosts to add multiple vehicles to their inventory with no restrictions on year, make, or model.

- **Tenet** (tenet.com/partner/turo) offers financing for electronic vehicles (EVs) only for Turo hosts looking to finance EVs. Hosts can pre-qualify quickly online with the ability to finance multiple vehicles over time. Tenet finances the purchase of new or used EVs, refinances current EVs to lower your monthly payments, and also provides lease buyout financing for your current EVs.

- **Westlake Fleet** (www.westlakefinancial.com/turo-new/)offers qualifying hosts with registered businesses (LLC, C-Corp, S-Corp or Partnership) lease financing up to $500,000 to grow their fleet and add up to 10 vehicles.

- **America First Credit Union** (www.americafirst.com/loans/vehicle-loans/turo-loans.html), the second largest credit union in the United States, is offering financing to qualifying Turo hosts in Arizona, Colorado, New Mexico, Nevada, and Utah. Hosts can apply either under their own name or as a registered business. Hosts with three or more vehicles on Turo must open a business account with the credit union to apply for business financing.

Insuring Your Vehicles

One of the most critical aspects of running a successful Turo car rental business is ensuring that your vehicles are adequately insured. As an entrepreneur in the Turo car rental niche, it is essential to understand the various insurance options available to protect your assets and your business.

When it comes to insuring your vehicles for Turo rentals, there are several key considerations to keep in mind. First and foremost, it is crucial to have the right type of insurance coverage in place to protect your vehicles and your business in the event of an accident or damage.

One option to consider is commercial insurance, which is specifically designed for businesses that rent out vehicles. Commercial insurance provides coverage for liability, physical damage, and other risks that may arise during Turo rentals. By investing in commercial insurance, you can protect your business against potential financial losses and legal liabilities.

Another essential insurance consideration for Turo car rental entrepreneurs is obtaining the proper coverage for your vehicles when they are not being rented out. Comprehensive insurance can provide coverage for theft, vandalism, and other non-rental related damages that may occur.

Additionally, it is important to review and understand the insurance requirements set forth by Turo, as they may have specific coverage requirements for vehicles listed on their platform. By ensuring that your vehicles meet Turo's insurance standards, you can avoid potential issues and ensure that your rentals are covered in the event of an accident.

I personally have had good experiences insuring my rental fleet with Lula (www.Lularentals.com). Lula offers comprehensive commercial auto insurance at reasonable rates.

Turo has partnered with American Business Insurance (ABI) to offer vehicle insurance designed to work hand-in-hand with Turo. ABI offers comprehensive commercial vehicle insurance, starting at $89 per car, per month, created to cover Turo hosts when the cars aren't on trips to make sure you're not double-paying for coverage.

Turo offers hosts insurance plans to cover the vehicles while they are on trips. The cost of the insurance is deducted from the host's trip revenue. All Turo hosts choose the protection plan that works best for them, and every host plan comes standard with $750,000* in third-party liability insurance from Travelers. Hosts can choose from five insurance coverage plans, each of which offers reimbursement for car repairs up to your car's actual cash value in case of damage during a trip.

In conclusion, insuring your vehicles is a crucial step in launching and maintaining a successful Turo car rental business. By investing in the right insurance coverage for your vehicles, you can protect your assets, your business, and your customers, ultimately setting yourself up for success in the competitive Turo car rental market.

Maintaining Your Fleet for Optimal Performance

As an entrepreneur in the Turo car rental business, one of the keys to success is maintaining your fleet for optimal performance. Ensuring that your vehicles are well-maintained not only enhances the safety and comfort of your customers but also prolongs the lifespan of your vehicles, ultimately saving you money in the long run.

Regular maintenance checks are essential to keep your fleet running smoothly. This includes routine oil changes, tire rotations, and brake inspections. By staying on top of these maintenance tasks, you can prevent costly repairs down the line and keep your vehicles in top condition.

In addition to routine maintenance, it's important to address any issues that arise promptly. Whether it's a strange noise coming from the engine or a warning light on the dashboard, ignoring potential problems can lead to bigger issues in the future. By addressing these issues early on, you can avoid costly repairs and keep your fleet operating at its best.

Another key aspect of maintaining your fleet is keeping your vehicles clean both inside and out. Regularly washing and detailing your vehicles not only enhances their appearance but also helps to prevent rust and corrosion. A clean and well-maintained vehicle is more likely to attract customers and leave a positive impression on them.

I recommend partnering with local detail shops, oil change shops and mechanic shops to ensure your vehicles are well maintained and meet your guests' standards.

Turo has partnered with the following vendors
to offer deals and discounts on vehicle safety
inspections, vehicle cleaning, and
maintenance:

Safety Inspections
- **Rideshare Mechanic**
  (ridesharemechanic.com/turo)
- **Andgo by Goodyear**
  (www.andgonow.com/turo-inspections)
- **Yoshi vehicle inspections**
  (www.yoshimobility.com/order/turo/inspe
  ctions)
- **Yourmechanic Yoshi mobile inspections**
  (www.yoshimobility.com/order/turo/inspe
  ctions)

Cleaning
- **Spiffy Smart Tumbler**
  (www.getspiffy.com/smarttumbler/turo-
  order)
- **Simply Clean**
  (www.simplycleanmobile.com)
- **Spiffy cleaning services**
  (www.getspiffy.com/turo)

Maintenance

- **Safelite** (www.safelite.com)
- **Jiffy Lube** (www.jiffylube.com/locations)
- **Caradvise** (caradvise.com/turo)
- **Wrench** (wrench.com/?promo=turo)
- **Openbay** (app.openbay.com/plus/turo/host)
- **Take 5 Oil Change** (www.take5.com/locations)
- **Spiffy maintenance** (www.getspiffy.com/turo)

By prioritizing maintenance and cleanliness in your fleet, you can ensure that your vehicles are always in top condition and ready to be rented out to customers. Taking care of your fleet not only benefits your business but also enhances the overall customer experience, leading to repeat business and positive reviews. Remember, a well-maintained fleet is a successful fleet.

Chapter 4: Marketing and Promoting Your Turo Car Rental Business

Utilizing Social Media to Reach Potential Customers

In today's digital age, utilizing social media is crucial for reaching potential customers and growing your Turo car rental business. Social media platforms such as Facebook, Instagram, and Twitter provide a direct line of communication with your target audience, allowing you to engage with them in real-time and build brand awareness.

One of the most important aspects of using social media for your Turo car rental business is creating a strong online presence. This means regularly posting engaging content, such as photos and videos of your fleet of cars, customer testimonials, and special promotions. By consistently updating your social media accounts, you can keep your followers informed about your business and entice them to book a rental.

Another effective strategy for reaching potential customers on social media is running targeted advertising campaigns. Platforms like Facebook and Instagram offer advanced targeting options that allow you to reach users based on their demographics, interests, and online behavior. By tailoring your ads to specific audiences, you can maximize the effectiveness of your marketing efforts and attract more customers to your Turo car rental business.

Additionally, social media can be a valuable tool for building relationships with your customers and providing excellent customer service. Responding to inquiries and feedback in a timely manner shows that you care about your customers and their experience with your business. By engaging with users on social media, you can foster loyalty and turn satisfied customers into repeat renters.

Overall, leveraging social media to reach potential customers is essential for growing your Turo car rental business. By creating a strong online presence, running targeted advertising campaigns, and providing excellent customer service, you can attract more customers and drive success for your business.

Partnering with Local Businesses for Promotion

Partnering with local businesses for promotion can be a strategic move to boost the visibility and success of your Turo car rental business. By collaborating with complementary businesses in your area, you can tap into their customer base and reach a wider audience. Here are some tips on how to effectively partner with local businesses for promotion:

1. Identify potential partners: Look for businesses that cater to a similar target market as your Turo car rental business. This could include hotels, travel agencies, car dealerships, or event planners. Reach out to them and pitch the idea of a collaboration.

2. Offer incentives: To entice local businesses to promote your Turo car rental services, consider offering them incentives such as discounted rates on car rentals for their customers or a referral bonus for every customer they send your way.

3. Cross-promote: Collaborate with local businesses on joint marketing initiatives such as co-hosting events, running promotions, or sharing each other's social media posts. This can help both businesses reach a larger audience and drive more traffic to your Turo car rental business.

4. Leverage partnerships for PR opportunities: Partnering with local businesses can also open up opportunities for PR, such as being featured in their newsletters, blogs, or social media channels. This can help boost your brand awareness and credibility in the local community.

5. Measure success: Track the results of your partnerships to see what is working and what is not. Monitor metrics such as website traffic, bookings, and customer feedback to determine the effectiveness of your collaborations.

By partnering with local businesses for promotion, you can create mutually beneficial relationships that help grow your Turo car rental business and establish a strong presence in your community.

Implementing a Referral Program for Repeat Customers

One of the key strategies to grow your Turo car rental business is to leverage the power of repeat customers through a referral program. By encouraging your satisfied customers to refer their friends and family to your business, you can tap into a new source of potential customers while rewarding your loyal clients at the same time.

To implement a successful referral program for repeat customers, start by identifying your most loyal clients who have consistently rented from you in the past. Reach out to them personally and thank them for their business, letting them know that you value their support. Inform them about the referral program and the rewards they can earn for each new customer they bring to your business.

Next, create a simple and easy-to-understand referral process that outlines the steps for customers to refer their contacts to your business. This could include sharing a unique referral link, code, or simply mentioning their name when booking a rental. Make sure to clearly communicate the rewards they can earn, whether it's a discount on their next rental or a free upgrade.

Promote your referral program through your website, social media channels, and email newsletters to reach a wider audience of potential referrers. Consider offering incentives for both the referrer and the new customer, such as a discount or bonus for both parties when a referral is successful.

By implementing a referral program for repeat customers, you can increase customer loyalty, drive word-of-mouth marketing, and attract new clients to your Turo car rental business. Don't miss out on this valuable opportunity to grow your business and reward your most loyal customers.

Advertise Online

Online advertising is not limited to established businesses. There are various online platforms where you can list your car to increase its visibility. Google Places, for instance, can put your car on the map by using your listing's custom URL. Similarly, FourSquare allows you to register your business to increase traffic, while Nextdoor offers the option to post your listing.

The Waze app, which provides real-time traffic and navigation updates, is an excellent platform to advertise your car as it makes it visible to drivers near your location.

Word of Mouth Promoting

Utilizing word of mouth can serve as a powerful form of advertising at virtually no cost. By leveraging this organic spread of information, potential customers will already be familiar with your car rental service when the need arises. Here's how to generate buzz around your listing:

- Incorporate your listing's URL and details into your email signatures.
- Encourage friends and family to share information about your service with their networks.
- Advertise your listing on local platforms such as neighborhood Facebook groups or online bulletin boards.
- Collect referrals and testimonials from satisfied customers to showcase the quality and reliability of your service.

Localize Your Advertising Efforts

While a significant portion of your potential guests may be traveling from distant locations, it's essential not to overlook those who reside right in your own neighborhood. Some locals may require your car rental service for various reasons, such as a weekend getaway or moving purposes. These individuals represent a valuable segment of your target audience.

To target local residents effectively, consider implementing the following strategy: Create flyers or door hangers featuring a QR code linked directly to your listing's URL. Distribute these promotional materials throughout your neighborhood to increase visibility and attract potential customers within your immediate vicinity.

Chapter 5: Managing Your Turo Car Rental Business

Handling Bookings and Inquiries

Handling bookings and inquiries is a crucial aspect of running a successful Turo car rental business. As an entrepreneur in this niche, it is essential to have efficient processes in place to ensure a seamless experience for both hosts and guests.

One of the first steps in handling bookings and inquiries is to establish clear and concise communication channels. Make sure to respond to inquiries promptly and provide detailed information about your vehicles, pricing, and any additional services you offer. This will help build trust with potential guests and increase the likelihood of securing bookings.

Once a booking is confirmed, it is important to have a system in place to manage reservations and keep track of availability. Consider using a booking management software to streamline this process and avoid double bookings. Additionally, having a clear cancellation policy in place will help protect your business and ensure that you are compensated for any lost revenue due to cancellations.

When it comes to handling inquiries, be prepared to answer questions about your vehicles, insurance coverage, and any specific requirements you may have for guests. Providing excellent customer service and being transparent about your policies will help you build a positive reputation in the Turo community.

In conclusion, handling bookings and inquiries effectively is key to the success of your Turo car rental business. By establishing clear communication channels, managing reservations efficiently, and providing excellent customer service, you can attract more guests and grow your business in this competitive market.

Managing Payments and Finances

In the world of Turo car rental business, managing payments and finances is crucial to the success and sustainability of your venture. As an entrepreneur in this niche market, it is essential to have a solid understanding of how to effectively handle the financial aspects of your business to ensure profitability and growth.

One of the first steps in managing payments and finances for your Turo car rental business is to set up a system for collecting payments from your customers. Whether you choose to use an online payment platform, such as PayPal or Stripe, or accept cash payments in person, it is important to have a streamlined process in place to ensure that payments are collected in a timely manner.

Additionally, keeping track of your expenses and revenues is essential for monitoring the financial health of your business. By maintaining detailed records of all income and expenses, you will be able to accurately assess your profitability and make informed decisions about pricing, marketing, and other business strategies.

Another important aspect of managing payments and finances in your Turo car rental business is setting aside a portion of your earnings for taxes. As a business owner, you will be responsible for paying taxes on your income, so it is important to plan ahead and save accordingly to avoid any surprises come tax season.

Overall, by implementing sound financial management practices, such as setting up a payment system, tracking expenses and revenues, and saving for taxes, you can ensure the long-term success of your Turo car rental business. Remember, managing payments and finances is a key component of running a successful business, so take the time to establish solid financial practices from the start.

Dealing with Customer Feedback and Reviews

Dealing with customer feedback and reviews is a crucial aspect of running a successful Turo car rental business. In the fast-paced world of entrepreneurship, it is important to stay ahead of the competition by providing exceptional customer service and addressing any concerns or issues promptly.

One of the first steps in handling customer feedback is to actively seek it out. Encourage customers to leave reviews and feedback after their rental experience, whether it be through email surveys or on your website. By proactively seeking feedback, you can gain valuable insights into what is working well and what areas may need improvement.

When it comes to negative reviews, it is important to respond in a timely and professional manner. Address the customer's concerns and offer a solution or compensation if necessary. By showing that you value customer feedback and are willing to make things right, you can turn a negative experience into a positive one and potentially retain that customer for future rentals.

On the other hand, positive reviews should also be acknowledged and appreciated. Thank customers for their feedback and let them know that their satisfaction is important to you. Positive reviews can help build credibility and attract new customers to your Turo car rental business.

In addition to responding to individual reviews, it is important to analyze feedback trends and make improvements to your business based on common themes. Whether it be improving communication with customers, upgrading your fleet of vehicles, or enhancing the rental experience, customer feedback can provide valuable insights that can help your business thrive.

Overall, dealing with customer feedback and reviews is an essential part of running a successful Turo car rental business. By actively seeking feedback, responding to reviews in a professional manner, and making improvements based on customer input, you can differentiate your business from the competition and build a loyal customer base.

Chapter 6: Scaling Your Turo Car Rental Business

Expanding Your Fleet and Reach

Once you have successfully launched your Turo car rental business and have a steady stream of bookings coming in, it may be time to consider expanding your fleet and reach. This chapter will guide you through the process of scaling up your business to reach new heights.

1. Assess Your Current Fleet: Before expanding, take a close look at your current fleet of vehicles. Are there any gaps in the types of cars you offer? Are there any popular models that you are missing out on? Conduct market research to identify the most in-demand vehicles in your area and consider adding them to your fleet. In Chapter 3, we discussed the vehicle dealers and manufacturers that have partnered with Turo to offer vehicle purchasing to its hosts.

2. Secure Financing: Expanding your fleet will require a significant investment in new vehicles. Explore financing options such as loans, lines of credit, or partnerships with investors to fund your expansion. Calculate the projected return on investment for each new vehicle to ensure that it is a sound financial decision.   In Chapter 3, we discussed the financial institutions that have partnered with Turo to offer vehicle financing to its hosts.

3. Expand Your Reach: In addition to growing your fleet, consider expanding your reach to new markets. Research other cities or regions where there is a high demand for car rentals and explore opportunities to establish a presence there. This could involve setting up new pickup locations, partnering with local businesses, or running targeted marketing campaigns.

4. Streamline Operations: As your fleet and reach grow, it is important to streamline your operations to ensure efficiency and profitability. Invest in tools and software that can help you manage a larger fleet, track bookings, and communicate with customers. Consider hiring additional staff to handle the increased workload and provide top-notch customer service.

By following these steps, you can successfully expand your Turo car rental business and take it to the next level. Keep your finger on the pulse of the market, stay adaptable, and continue to innovate to stay ahead of the competition. The sky's the limit for your business, so dream big and drive forward with confidence.

Hiring Staff to Help Manage Operations

As your Turo car rental business grows, you may find yourself overwhelmed with the day-to-day operations. Hiring staff to help manage these operations can be a crucial step in ensuring the success and scalability of your business. In this subchapter, we will discuss the importance of hiring staff, the qualities to look for in potential hires, and how to effectively onboard and train new employees.

One of the main reasons to hire staff is to free up your time as an entrepreneur to focus on growing and expanding your business. By delegating tasks to qualified individuals, you can ensure that the daily operations of your Turo car rental business run smoothly and efficiently. This will also allow you to take on more clients and increase your revenue stream.

When hiring staff for your Turo car rental business, it is important to look for individuals who are reliable, trustworthy, and have a strong work ethic. Since they will be representing your brand and interacting with customers, it is crucial that they are professional and courteous at all times. Additionally, they should have a good understanding of the Turo platform and be able to effectively communicate with clients to address any issues or concerns.

Once you have hired new staff members, it is essential to provide them with thorough training and onboarding to ensure they are equipped to handle their responsibilities. This may include shadowing experienced employees, providing hands-on training, and offering resources for ongoing learning and development.

In conclusion, hiring staff to help manage operations in your Turo car rental business can be a game-changer in terms of efficiency and growth. By investing in the right team members and providing them with the necessary training and support, you can take your business to the next level and achieve even greater success.

Diversifying Your Services to Increase Revenue

As an entrepreneur in the Turo car rental business, it's crucial to find ways to diversify your services in order to increase revenue and stay competitive in the market. By offering a variety of services and options to your customers, you can attract a wider range of clients and maximize your earning potential.

One way to diversify your services is to offer different types of vehicles for rent. While starting with a few popular models is a good way to establish your business, expanding your fleet to include luxury cars, SUVs, or even specialty vehicles like convertibles or electric cars can appeal to a wider range of customers. By catering to different preferences and needs, you can attract more bookings and increase your revenue stream.

Another way to diversify your services is to offer additional amenities or packages to enhance the rental experience for your customers. This could include options like car delivery and pick-up, GPS navigation systems, child car seats, or even roadside assistance services. By providing these added conveniences, you can differentiate your business from competitors and attract customers who are willing to pay more for a premium experience.

Additionally, consider expanding your services beyond traditional car rentals. You could offer services like long-term rentals, corporate rental packages, or even event rentals for weddings or special occasions. By tapping into different market segments and offering specialized services, you can increase your revenue potential and create new opportunities for growth.

In conclusion, diversifying your services in the Turo car rental business is essential for increasing revenue and staying ahead of the competition. By offering a variety of vehicles, amenities, and specialized rental options, you can attract a broader customer base and maximize your earning potential. Stay innovative and open to new ideas to keep your business thriving and profitable.

Chapter 7: Legal and Compliance Considerations for Your Turo Car Rental Business

Understanding Turo's Terms and Conditions

As entrepreneurs looking to launch a Turo car rental business, it is crucial to thoroughly understand and abide by Turo's terms and conditions. These terms and conditions outline the rules and regulations that govern the use of the platform and are essential to ensuring a smooth and successful operation.

One key aspect of Turo's terms and conditions is the eligibility requirements for both hosts and guests. Hosts must meet certain criteria, such as having a valid driver's license and insurance coverage, in order to list their cars on the platform. Guests, on the other hand, must also meet certain requirements, such as having a clean driving record and being of a certain age, in order to rent a car through Turo.

Another important aspect of Turo's terms and conditions is the insurance coverage provided by the platform. Turo offers a $1 million liability insurance policy to hosts, which provides coverage in the event of an accident or damage to the car while it is being rented out. Hosts should familiarize themselves with the details of this policy to ensure they are adequately protected.

Additionally, Turo's terms and conditions outline the rules and regulations regarding pricing, cancellations, and disputes between hosts and guests. It is important for entrepreneurs to understand these rules in order to avoid any potential conflicts or misunderstandings that may arise during the rental process.

By taking the time to thoroughly understand and comply with Turo's terms and conditions, entrepreneurs can ensure a successful and profitable Turo car rental business. Adhering to these guidelines will help to build trust with both hosts and guests, leading to positive reviews and repeat business in the future.

Obtaining Necessary Licenses and Permits

One of the most crucial steps in launching your Turo car rental business is obtaining the necessary licenses and permits. As an entrepreneur looking to enter the Turo car rental niche, it is essential to ensure that you are operating legally and in compliance with all regulations.

First and foremost, you will need to obtain a business license to operate your Turo car rental business. This license will allow you to legally conduct business in your area and will vary depending on your location. Be sure to research the specific requirements for obtaining a business license in your city or state.

Additionally, you will need to obtain any specific permits required to operate a car rental business. Some areas may require special permits for businesses that rent out vehicles, so it is important to check with your local government to determine what permits you will need to secure.

Another important consideration is insurance. As a Turo car rental business owner, you will need to have the appropriate insurance coverage to protect yourself, your vehicles, and your customers. Make sure to research the insurance requirements for car rental businesses in your area and secure the necessary coverage.

Lastly, it is important to stay up to date on any changes to regulations or requirements for operating a Turo car rental business. Regulations can vary by location and may change over time, so it is crucial to stay informed and ensure that your business remains in compliance.

By obtaining the necessary licenses and permits for your Turo car rental business, you can operate legally and protect yourself and your customers. Make sure to do your research, follow the proper steps, and stay informed to set your business up for success.

Most states have a motor vehicle commission that regulates licensing requirements in their state. Please be sure to contact your local motor vehicle commission for specific regulations or licensing requirements in your state.

Ensuring Compliance with Insurance Regulations

Ensuring compliance with insurance regulations is crucial for entrepreneurs in the Turo car rental business. Failure to adhere to these regulations can result in hefty fines, legal troubles, and even the closure of your business. Therefore, it is essential to familiarize yourself with the insurance requirements specific to your state and the Turo platform.

One of the first steps in ensuring compliance with insurance regulations is to thoroughly read and understand the terms and conditions set forth by Turo. This will give you a clear understanding of the insurance coverage provided by the platform and any additional insurance requirements you need to meet.

It is also important to work closely with an insurance provider that specializes in rental car insurance. They can help you navigate the complex world of insurance regulations and ensure that you have the appropriate coverage for your Turo car rental business. Make sure to review your insurance policy regularly to ensure that it meets all necessary requirements and provides adequate coverage for your vehicles and customers.

Additionally, staying up to date on any changes to insurance regulations in your state is essential. Laws and regulations regarding rental car insurance can vary from state to state, so it is important to stay informed and make any necessary adjustments to your insurance policy accordingly.

By ensuring compliance with insurance regulations, you can protect your business, your customers, and yourself from potential risks and liabilities. Taking the time to understand and meet these regulations will set your Turo car rental business up for success in the long run.

In Chapter 3, we made note of insurance providers who are experienced in providing commercial insurance that meets the required thresholds in most states.

Chapter 8: Troubleshooting Common Issues in Your Turo Car Rental Business

Dealing with Cancellations and No-Shows

Dealing with cancellations and no-shows is an inevitable part of running a Turo car rental business. While it can be frustrating and disruptive to your operations, there are strategies you can implement to minimize the impact and ensure smooth operations.

First and foremost, it is crucial to have a clear and concise cancellation policy in place. Make sure your customers are aware of your policy before they book a car through your platform. This will help set expectations and reduce the likelihood of last-minute cancellations.

In the event of a cancellation, it is important to have a plan in place to fill the vacancy left by the canceled reservation. Consider offering last-minute deals or discounts to attract new customers and ensure that your cars are being utilized to their full potential.

No-shows can be even more challenging to deal with, as they can result in lost revenue and wasted resources. To mitigate the impact of no-shows, consider implementing a prepayment or deposit policy for reservations. This will incentivize customers to show up or cancel in a timely manner.

Additionally, consider implementing a penalty fee for customers who fail to show up for their reservation without notice. This will help deter no-shows and compensate for any lost revenue.

Overall, dealing with cancellations and no-shows is an inevitable part of running a Turo car rental business. By having a clear cancellation policy, implementing strategies to fill vacancies, and penalizing no-shows, you can minimize the impact on your business and ensure smooth operations.

Handling Vehicle Damage and Maintenance Disputes

One of the inevitable challenges that entrepreneurs in the Turo car rental business may face is dealing with vehicle damage and maintenance disputes. It is crucial to have a clear protocol in place to address these issues effectively and ensure the smooth operation of your business.

First and foremost, it is essential to have a detailed inspection process in place before and after each rental. This includes documenting the condition of the vehicle, taking photos, and noting any existing damage. By having this thorough documentation, you can easily determine whether any new damage occurred during the rental period.

In the event of vehicle damage, it is important to communicate with the renter promptly and professionally. Provide them with the necessary information on how to report the damage and follow up with them to gather more details. Having open and transparent communication can help resolve disputes quickly and amicably.

When it comes to maintenance disputes, it is essential to have a clear understanding of your responsibilities as a car rental business owner. Make sure to follow the manufacturer's recommended maintenance schedule and keep detailed records of all maintenance and repairs. This will not only ensure the safety and reliability of your vehicles but also protect you in case of any disputes.

In case of disagreements with renters regarding damage or maintenance issues, consider involving a third party mediator or arbitrator. This can help facilitate a fair and impartial resolution that satisfies both parties.

By having a proactive approach to handling vehicle damage and maintenance disputes, you can maintain the reputation of your Turo car rental business and ensure the satisfaction of your customers. Remember that clear communication, thorough documentation, and a willingness to resolve conflicts can go a long way in building a successful and sustainable business.

Resolving Customer Complaints and Disputes

As entrepreneurs in the Turo car rental business, it is crucial to understand the importance of resolving customer complaints and disputes in a timely and effective manner. Customer satisfaction is key to the success of your business, and handling complaints professionally can turn a negative experience into a positive one.

The first step in resolving customer complaints is to listen actively to their concerns. Allow customers to express their frustrations and grievances, and show empathy towards their situation. This will help build trust and rapport with the customer, demonstrating that you value their feedback and are committed to finding a resolution.

Once you have listened to the customer's concerns, it is important to take swift action to address the issue. Offer solutions that are fair and reasonable, and be willing to go above and beyond to make things right. This may involve offering a refund, providing a discount on future rentals, or taking steps to prevent the issue from happening again in the future.

In cases where a dispute arises between you and a customer, it is important to remain calm and professional. Avoid getting defensive or confrontational, and instead focus on finding a mutually beneficial solution. Consider involving a third party mediator if necessary, such as Turo customer support, to help facilitate a resolution.

By handling customer complaints and disputes with integrity and professionalism, you can build a positive reputation for your Turo car rental business and foster long-lasting relationships with your customers. Remember, a satisfied customer is more likely to become a repeat customer and recommend your business to others.

Chapter 9: Maximizing Profit and Growth in Your Turo Car Rental Business

Analyzing Performance Metrics to Identify Opportunities for Growth

As entrepreneurs in the Turo car rental business, it is crucial to continuously monitor and analyze performance metrics to identify opportunities for growth. By understanding key indicators of success, you can make informed decisions that will drive your business forward.

One of the most important performance metrics to track is revenue. By analyzing your revenue streams, you can identify which cars are generating the most income and which ones may need to be reevaluated or removed from your fleet. Additionally, tracking revenue can help you identify trends in customer demand and adjust your pricing strategy accordingly.

Another key metric to monitor is utilization rate. This metric measures the percentage of time your cars are being rented out compared to the total available time. A high utilization rate indicates that your fleet is in high demand, while a low rate may signal the need to adjust your marketing or pricing strategies to attract more customers.

Customer satisfaction is also a critical metric to track. By collecting feedback from renters, you can identify areas for improvement and make changes to enhance the customer experience. Happy customers are more likely to return and recommend your services to others, leading to increased revenue and growth opportunities.

In addition to these key metrics, it is important to analyze other factors such as marketing effectiveness, operational efficiency, and competition in the market. By taking a comprehensive approach to performance analysis, you can identify opportunities for growth and make strategic decisions that will propel your Turo car rental business to success.

Implementing Strategies to Increase Bookings and Revenue

As entrepreneurs in the Turo car rental business, it is crucial to continuously implement strategies that will help increase bookings and revenue for your business. In this subchapter, we will explore some effective tactics to attract more customers and boost your profits.

One key strategy is to optimize your online presence. Make sure your Turo listings are attractive and include high-quality photos of your vehicles. Utilize keywords and descriptions that will help your listings appear in relevant searches. Consider offering promotions or discounts to attract new customers and encourage repeat bookings.

Another important strategy is to establish partnerships with local businesses or tourism agencies. Collaborating with hotels, airlines, or event organizers can help you reach a wider audience and attract more customers. Consider offering exclusive deals or packages for their customers to entice them to book with your Turo business.

Furthermore, consider expanding your fleet to offer a wider range of vehicles to cater to different customer needs. Conduct market research to identify popular car models or trends in your area and invest in vehicles that will attract more bookings. You can also consider offering additional services such as car delivery or pickup to enhance the customer experience and differentiate your business from competitors.

In conclusion, by implementing these strategies and continuously monitoring and adjusting your approach, you can effectively increase bookings and revenue for your Turo car rental business. Stay proactive and innovative in your marketing efforts to stay ahead in this competitive industry.

Planning for the Future: Expanding Your Turo Empire

As an entrepreneur in the Turo car rental business, it's essential to always be thinking ahead and planning for the future growth of your empire. Expanding your Turo business can lead to increased profits, greater market share, and a more robust brand presence. Here are some key tips to help you plan for the future expansion of your Turo empire:

1. Set clear goals: Before you can expand your Turo business, you need to have a clear vision of where you want to go. Set specific goals for growth, such as increasing your fleet size, expanding into new markets, or reaching a certain revenue target. Having concrete goals will help guide your decision-making and keep you focused on your long-term vision.

2. Develop a detailed expansion plan: Once you have your goals in place, it's important to create a detailed plan for how you will achieve them. Consider factors such as funding, staffing, marketing, and logistics as you map out your expansion strategy. Having a well-thought-out plan will help you stay organized and on track as you grow your Turo empire.

3. Invest in technology: To support the expansion of your Turo business, consider investing in technology that can help streamline your operations and improve the customer experience. This could include software for managing reservations, GPS tracking for your vehicles, or a mobile app for customers to book rentals on the go. By leveraging technology, you can scale your business more efficiently and effectively.

4. Build strategic partnerships: As you look to expand your Turo empire, consider forming strategic partnerships with other businesses in the industry. This could include collaborations with car dealerships, auto repair shops, or travel agencies to help attract new customers and drive growth. By building strong partnerships, you can leverage the resources and expertise of others to accelerate your expansion efforts.

Conclusion

This book has equipped you with a comprehensive roadmap for navigating the intricate landscape of launching and managing a successful Turo car rental business. Throughout the book, we've delved into every aspect of the process including setting up your account, creating compelling listings, sourcing vehicles, financing vehicles, insuring vehicles, optimizing pricing strategies, hiring staff and providing exceptional customer service. By following the practical advice and expert insights provided, entrepreneurs are empowered to overcome challenges, seize opportunities, and drive their Turo businesses toward success.

As readers embark on their journey from start-up to speed, they are armed with the knowledge, tools, and confidence needed to thrive in the dynamic world of peer-to-peer car rentals. With dedication, perseverance, and the guidance offered within these pages, the sky is truly the limit for aspiring Turo hosts ready to make their mark in the industry.

Remember, the key to expanding your Turo empire is to stay focused, set clear goals, and be willing to adapt and evolve as you grow. With the right strategy and mindset, the sky's the limit for your Turo business.